Edexcel Economics A
Theme 3: Business Behaviour and the Labour Market

By

Brendan Casey

ISBN 978 1535589406

Table of Contents

About the author

The author is Head of Economics at Ashbourne Independent Sixth Form College in London, and is a graduate of the London School of Economics. He has been teaching the Edexcel A level economics syllabus for 15 years, and has also been an examiner for this syllabus.

Types of firms

1

1.1 Distinction between public sector and private sector organisations

Private sector organisations - these are firms which are owned either by shareholders or private individuals, e.g. sole traders, partnerships. Firms which are owned by shareholders, can either be private limited companies or public limited companies. Private limited companies have the letters 'ltd' after their name, e.g. Virgin Ltd, whereas public limited companies have the letters 'plc' after their name, e.g. Tesco plc. Only the shares of plc's are available on the stock market.

Public sector organisations - these are organisations that are controlled by the government e.g. NHS, education. Their purpose is to provide a service to the public.

1.2 The divorce of ownership from control: the principal-agent problem

The divorce of ownership from control means that one group of people own the company, but another group of people run the company on a day-to-day basis. We see this in limited companies: the shareholders own the company but the directors and managers run it on a day-to-day basis. This gives rise to what's known as the 'principal-agent problem'. This means the agents, i.e. directors and managers, may not always make decisions in the best interests of the shareholders, i.e. the principal. For example, instead of maximising profits they might maximise sales because they know their bonuses depend on it; directors could award themselves big pay rises because they know the shareholders are unlikely to challenge it.

Sole traders and partnerships can also have this problem if they grow to a size where day-to-day running of the business is delegated to managers who could have different objectives to the owners, e.g. have an easy life, maximise bonuses.

1.3 Distinction between profit and not-for-profit organisations

Types of firms

Not-for-profit organisations comprise mainly charities, e.g. Oxfam. Their objective is to use any surplus they generate in pursuit of their goals.

All organisations in the private sector are profit-making organisations and the objective is to maximise the return to shareholders or the owner.

Economies of scale

2

2.1 Economies of scale (EOS)

Economies of scale are the factors which cause average cost to fall as output rises. They can be split into internal and external economies of scale:

Internal – these benefit only the firm:

- **Purchasing economies** - this means the bulk buying of raw materials and components. The more you buy, the bigger the discount you get from suppliers therefore average cost falls.
- **Technical economies** - this means replacing labour with capital (plant and machinery). Large firms can go out and buy the latest plant and machinery and reduce average costs.
- **Financial economies** - large firms get lower rates of interest from banks because they borrow more and seem a better risk.
- **Marketing economies** - large firms can spread their advertising and promotional costs over a large number of units. They can also cross sell their products.
- **Managerial economies** – as firms grow managers can specialise in their job functions and get more expert at their jobs, e.g. sales, production, finance. This raises productivity and reduces average costs.
- **Increased dimensions** – this has different applications. One is that it reduces transport costs because it means firms can use bigger and bigger carriers, e.g. lorries, ships. Transport costs fall because there are less trips. Another example is warehousing; the bigger the warehouse the smaller the warehousing costs per unit.

External - these benefit the industry as a whole:

- **Access to pool of skilled labour** - this occurs when a significant part of the industry is located in one area, e.g. Midlands – car manufacturing, City of London – finance. It means less money needs to be spent on training and recruitment.

- **Lower component cost** - if large parts of an industry are located in one area it reduces the transport costs for suppliers. They can pass this cost saving on to the industry.
- **Breakthrough in research and development** - breakthrough in R&D by one company may lead to benefits for the whole industry, e.g. new materials, processor chips.

2.2 Diseconomies of scale (DEOS)

These are factors that cause average costs to rise as firms get bigger. There are three of them:

- **Co-ordination and communication** - as firms increase in size the amount of horizontal and vertical communication increases. More and more meetings take place to co-ordinate the workings of the various departments. This increases management and administration costs.
- **Motivation** - employees in large organisations may find it hard to feel part of a team. Therefore productivity may suffer and average costs rise.
- **Transport costs** - large companies with large supplier networks may find transport costs rise if they are far away from suppliers.

2.3 Diagram of economies and diseconomies of scale

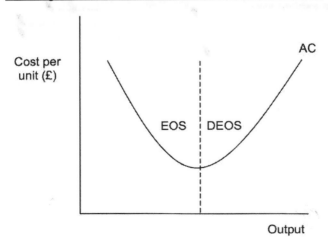

The birth and growth of firms

3

3.1 Measuring the size of a firm

This can be done in four ways:

- Turnover – amount of sales.
- Market share – measured by either sales turnover or volume of units.
- Capital employed – the amount of money invested in the business.
- Number of employees.

3.2 Constraints on growth

(i) Barriers to entry

Barriers to entry are factors that prevent new firms from entering a market. The main ones are:

- Initial capital costs, e.g. plant and machinery, factories
- Marketing and branding – brand loyalty means its difficult for new firms to break into a market. Significant amounts of money may have to be spent on advertising for a firm to establish themselves in the market.
- Economies of scale – a new firm may have to sell very large volumes of a product before it can achieve the sort of average cost the existing firms already have.
- Limit pricing – this means the existing firms setting prices below the average costs of potential new entrants therefore deterring them from entering the market.
- Patents – patents give a firm a legal monopoly for 25 years. No one else is able to make the product without their permission. They are an important limit on growth in scientific and technical industries. Having said this, they can be good for firms and the economy as a whole, because they incentivise research and development and make sure firms are properly rewarded for putting in their investment.

Evaluation

Initial costs - big firms may not see this as a problem. They have the financial resources to cope with it, e.g. Santander entered the UK banking sector in the 2000's.

Marketing and branding - big firms may already have a strong brand name, so again may not see this as a problem. Consumers are also getting more used to foreign brands because of globalisation, so foreign multi-nationals are less worried about the initial lack of brand recognition.

Economies of scale - big firms may be able to quickly establish supply chains to bring costs down. They may also have existing supply chains they can use, e.g. Aldi, Lidl in the supermarket sector.

Niche markets - within any industry there are always niche markets smaller players can exploit and so enter the market.

Trade cycle - e.g. recession. Existing firms can't control all factors. The financial crisis triggered a recession and period of low growth. Firms like Aldi and Lidl in the supermarket sector, have been able to exploit this and grow, by offering very competitive prices to consumers looking for a bargain. Incumbent firms like Tesco and Sainsbury have found this difficult to cope with and lost market share as a result.

Competition and Markets Authority - limit pricing is illegal, so firms can be fined if found guilty of using it. For further detail on the working of the Competition and Markets Authority see section 4.0.

(ii) Other constraints on growth

Legislation and regulation – the Competition Act outlaws restrictive trade practices such as price fixing, market sharing agreements and predatory pricing. The Competition and Markets Authority (CMA) investigates mergers where a firm will accumulate more than 25% market share. Mergers can only go ahead if the CMA is satisfied the new firm will not substantially reduce competition.

Size of the market - mass-market products require large companies, which can exploit economies of scale e.g. cars, computers, soft drinks. Niche market products only require small firms because the target market is much smaller, e.g. vintage cars. Therefore, the size of the market determines the size of the firms.

Access to finance - for firms to expand they need to access finance, e.g. bank loans. This is harder for small firms than big firms as they are seen as a bigger risk. It's also more costly for small firms as because of the perceived risk they get charged higher rates of interest.

Motive of the owner – some owners are content to run small businesses. They aren't interested in getting any bigger. The ambition of the owner is therefore a factor in determining the growth of a firm.

3.3 Reasons for the survival of small firms

Low barriers to entry - e.g.

- Economies of scale - it may not be that difficult to achieve full economies of scale, e.g. restaurants.
- Initial costs - some businesses have low initial costs and don't require large amounts of capital, e.g. plumber, electrician.
- Skill level - some businesses have a low skill level and do not require years of experience, e.g. window cleaner

Niche markets - some products have got small numbers of consumers. These don't attract large companies because profits are low.

Personal service - some customers prefer a personal service, small firms can exploit this and therefore stay in business.

Local monopoly power - location and convenience can mean that small businesses achieve local monopoly power, e.g. local supermarkets and newsagents. This allows them to stay in business even when they have big competitors close by.

Owner's preference - some businessmen are happy to stay small. They aren't interested in getting any bigger.

3.4 Reasons for growth

Higher profits - growth means higher profits. With higher profits a firm can invest more and build further barriers to entry, e.g. advertising and branding. This helps it to defend and build further market share. Higher profits also means higher rewards for shareholders, which makes it easier to attract further investment.

Economies of scale - growth means a firm can achieve further economies of scale. It lowers per unit costs and makes a firm more competitive. It also helps to protect profit margins.

Market power/price leadership - price leadership means that consumers perceive a firm's product as the top brand and all other firms (the 'price followers') have to adjust their prices according to what the price leader does. This gives the price leader power over pricing in the market and therefore over it's own and other firms' profit margins. Growth enhances the status of a firm and makes it more likely they can achieve price leadership.

Prestige - there's a certain amount of prestige in growing and being the biggest. It helps to increase sales and increase the likelihood they will be the market leader. Consumers trust big companies.

Diversification – by growing firms can enter new markets and develop new products. This helps to spread risk and make the firm more stable.

3.5 Types of growth

Firms can grow in two ways:

(i) Organic growth - this means growing by expanding your current market or finding new markets. It's also known as internal growth.

Advantages

- Firm is building on existing strengths and knows its own market
- Less risky than merging or taking over other firms

Disadvantages

- Slower way to grow than external growth
- Competition may limit ability to grow this way

(ii) External growth - this means growing by taking over or merging with other firms, e.g. horizontal integration, vertical integration.

3.6 Types of integration and mergers

3.6.1 Horizontal integration

This means two firms merging at the same stage of production or distribution e.g. two supermarkets merging.

Advantages

- **Economies of scale**, e.g.

  ➢ Purchasing economies – bigger discounts from suppliers.
  ➢ Financial economies – lower interest charges because the loans will be bigger
  ➢ Managerial economies – the merged company can pick and choose the best staff, cut costs by merging the two head offices and cut waste by removing duplication in the management structure
  ➢ Marketing economies – the marketing and advertising budget will be spread over a larger number of units, therefore the marketing costs per unit will fall.

- **Prestige** – there's a certain amount of prestige attached to being bigger. It enhances the firms reputation and attracts extra sales
- **It's a quick and easy way to grow** – it's much quicker than internal growth
- **Increase market share** – therefore it can make a firm a leading player in the market.

Disadvantages

- **Diseconomies of scale,** e.g.

  ➢ Communication and co-ordination – it may be difficult to merge the two management structures together and make the two companies work together as a single unit rather than two separate companies.
  ➢ Motivation – employees may lose their jobs and it may be hard to get everybody in the merged company to pull in the same direction. There may also be a clash of company cultures.

- **Job losses** – this could lead to high redundancy costs. It might also mean the firm loses valuable people without realising it.
- **Factory closure costs** – these could be more expensive than planned.

3.6.2 Vertical integration

This means two firms merging at different stages of production or distribution. There are two types:

(i) Backward vertical

This is where a firm takes over or merges with another firm at a previous stage of production or distribution, e.g. brewery taking over a hops farm

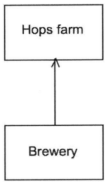

Advantages

- Firm can control quality and delivery times of supply.
- Creates a secure line of supply – therefore if there are shortages the firm will get preference.
- Supplier's profits now belong to the firm.

Disadvantages

- Secure outlet for the suppliers goods may make the supplier complacent – therefore quality, cost and delivery of goods may suffer in the long run.

(ii) Forward vertical

This is where a firm merges with or takes over another firm at the next stage of production or distribution, e.g. a brewery taking over a chain of pubs.

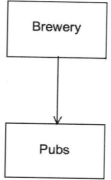

Advantages

- Creates a secure outlet for the firm's products - it means that only the firm's products can be sold in that retail outlet. This reduces competition and increases sales.
- Merchandising and display – the firm can control how products are displayed and therefore increase sales.
- The retailers profits now belong to the firm

Disadvantages

- Lack of choice in the retail outlets may mean lower sales.
- Firm may be more reluctant to try promotion methods like discounting and special offers to increase sales because they are more conscious of brand issues.

3.6.3 Conglomerate

This is when a firm merges and takes over businesses in unrelated industries, e.g. Unilever, Procter & Gamble.

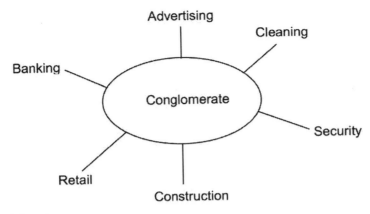
Birth and growth of firms

Advantages

- It spreads risk – even if one part of the economy is doing badly others may be doing well. It therefore means the business is better able to cope with fluctuations in the trade cycle.
- There may be a sharing of good practice among managers – therefore the overall quality of management improves.
- A firm may have reached saturation point in its current markets – it therefore gives it an opportunity to find new markets for expansion.

Disadvantages

- Communication and co-ordination may become a problem – because of the diverse nature of the business the senior management team may find it difficult to get everyone to pull in the same direction.
- Lack of knowledge of the new business sector - developing expertise takes time and it's difficult to find good managers. It's therefore not a strategy that's guaranteed to pay off.

3.7 Advantages and disadvantages of integration for consumers

(i) Horizontal integration

Advantages

- Lower prices – the merged firm can get bigger discounts from suppliers and therefore pass on the cost savings to consumers.
- More choice – the merged firm can use their combined knowledge to offer a better range of products to consumers.
- Better service – the merged firm can pick and choose the best staff. This should improve management quality and the quality of rank and file staff. If they are more profitable they can also put more money into training.

Disadvantages

- Higher prices – if a firm builds up a dominant position it may be tempted to raise its prices because it realises there is a lack of competition.
- Reduced choice – in order to maximise profits the merged firm may reduce choice. That way it can get bigger discounts from fewer lines.
- Lower quality products – the merged firm may reduce quality to cut costs because it knows it has a dominant market position.
- Lower quality service – the merged firm may lose its "personal touch". Employees may feel increasingly distant from the company and lose their sense of loyalty to the customers.

(ii) Backward vertical integration

Advantages

- May lead to better quality products – firms can control the quality of supplies.
- Customers are less likely to suffer from "stock-outs" – firm now controls the supply chain.
- Cheaper products – firms may pass on cost savings to consumers.

Disadvantages

- Reduced choice - firms control over the supply chain may mean they try to maximise profits by reducing choice.

- Supplier complacency – supplier may get complacent because they know they have a secure outlet for their goods therefore in the long-run costs rise, quality falls and consumers suffer.

(iii) Forward vertical integration

Advantages

- Quality of service should improve – staff will be more expert and be able to give better advice because the firm can give better training. Display and merchandising should also be of a higher quality
- Lower prices - prices may fall if the firm passes on cost savings to customers.

Disadvantages

- Reduced choice – firm may only stock the parent company's products.
- Higher prices – firm may use market power to put prices up.

3.8 Advantages and disadvantages of integration for employees

Advantages

- Improved job security – a bigger company has a better chance of survival, therefore job security should improve.
- More jobs – a bigger firm should be able to grow more quickly and create more jobs.
- Improved career path – for some employees there will be the opportunity for promotion and a better career path.

Disadvantages

- Loss of jobs – a merged company may cut costs by cutting back on labour costs. This could result in the loss of jobs.
- Lower morale – becoming part of a bigger firm may mean a firm loses its personal touch. Work relationships may get disrupted and motivation may suffer.

3.9 Demergers

Demerger means a firm splitting itself into two or more separate parts to create two or more separate businesses.

Reasons for demergers

Lack of synergies – demergers often occur because of the failure of a merger to produce the synergies expected. By synergies it's meant the belief that by combining two or more separate businesses the sum will be greater than its parts (2+2=5). Many mergers fail because they fail to deliver the cost savings and efficiencies hoped for. They can lead to diseconomies of scale rather than economies of scale.

To create better value for shareholders – by demerging the directors may be able to create extra value for shareholders. The weak performance of one part of the business can drag down the share price for the whole business. By demerging the directors can create a better deal for shareholders.

To create better focus for the business – the directors may feel by splitting the business into two or more parts each one will get better focus. This means they can deliver higher profits and growth for shareholders.

Impact of demergers on businesses, workers and consumers

Businesses - assuming the demerger is a success firms should be able to cut costs and increase profits. If they have a greater focus then they should become more innovative as well.

Workers - for workers the picture is mixed. For many workers it might mean they lose their jobs, but for others who to stay it might mean promotion or a clearer career path. In the long run it could mean greater job security as the firm refocuses and concentrates on what it does best.

Consumers - for consumers it should mean lower prices and better quality products if the firm passes on the cost savings, and also uses those cost savings for re-investment. On the other hand, it could mean little difference for them and the firm just pays out bigger dividends to the shareholders.

Competition policy in the UK

4

4.1 Purpose of competition policy

- To ensure there is free and fair competition in the market.
- To ensure a better allocation of resources and to prevent market failure, thereby promoting growth in the economy.
- To ensure consumer protection – i.e. lower prices, more choice and improved quality of products and services for consumers.

4.2 How competition policy is implemented

Competition policy in the UK is overseen by the Competition and Markets Authority (CMA). This replaced the Competition Commission and Office for Fair Trading in 2014. It uses the Competition Act (1998) and Enterprise Act (2002) as its framework. It has two main areas of operation:

- **Anti-competitive practices** – it investigates anti-competitive practices such as price fixing, market sharing agreements and predatory pricing. It can impose fines of up to 10% of a firm's turnover if it finds a firm guilty.
- **Takeovers and mergers** – if it feels there will be a 'substantial lessening of competition' it orders an investigation. This is automatic if the merger results in a firm with a market share greater than 25% or turnover greater than £70m. A market share of 25% or more is the legal definition of a monopoly.

4.3 The meaning of a 'substantial lessening of competition' in CMA investigations

In 2002 'substantial lessening of competition' replaced the old 'public interest' criterion, which was used to decide whether a merger or takeover could go ahead. Mostly this is assessed in terms of how the merger/takeover effects consumers in terms of price, choice and quality.

If the CMA feels there will be a 'substantial lessening of competition' then they can recommend the merger/takeover doesn't take place and/or require the firms to sell off part of their businesses to reduce their market share.

It's important to note that firms can have more than 25% market share but they have to demonstrate that competition won't be substantially effected.

4.4 Promotion of small and medium sized businesses (SMEs)

This is another way the government seeks to promote competition. SMEs provide about 60% of jobs and 50% of GDP in the UK, so they are vital to the economy. An SME is any business with less than 250 employees. Recent initiatives have been:

- Funding for Lending Scheme (FLS) - this put pressure on the banks to lend more money to SMEs if they wanted to benefit from QE.
- Grants and advice for young people who want to start their own business.
- A government pledge to spend one third of its contracts budget with SMEs by 2020, e.g. transport, education.

4.5 Reasons why competition policy may be ineffective

Asymmetric information - anti-competitive practices are difficult to prove without all the facts. Firms can limit the information they give to the CMA and therefore escape penalty. They can also cover-up wrong doing with plausible excuses, e.g. predatory pricing can be covered up as discounting.

Fines may not be high enough – some very profitable firms may just treat them as additional expenses.

Investigations/court cases can be lengthy – therefore it can take a long time to introduce market changes.

Regulatory capture - this means the firms in an industry influencing the regulator to such a degree that they get them to act in their own interests, e.g. collusion may be passed off as coincidence because firms have similar cost structures.

Government failure – the CMA can make mistakes, e.g. requiring a big firm to sell off part of their business and this subsequently having a negative effect on consumers, such as it meaning less investment will take place.

Lack of resources - the CMA only has limited resources in terms of finance and manpower. It can't investigate every case of market abuse. High profile cases tend to take precedence.

Lobbying - firms may have significant political power. They may also employ thousands of people. The CMA and government may feel under pressure to water-down legislation/regulation or back down on decisions if they think it will effect jobs or other businesses, e.g. banning cigarette displays in shops.

4.6 Government intervention to protect suppliers and employees

Suppliers - the government intervenes to protect suppliers from the monopsony power of buyers by promoting competition, legislation and the CMA, e.g. the CMA recently launched an investigation of supermarkets to see if they were exploiting their suppliers with low prices.

Employees - the government protects employees by employment law, health and safety law, and also the national minimum wage and national living wage, e.g. there are redundancy procedures firms must follow or they could be taken to an industrial tribunal.

4.7 Consumer welfare

Consumer welfare means the individual benefits derived from the consumption of a good or service. If you are asked about this in a question think about price, choice and quality.

Theory of the firm

5

5.1 Input

Inputs to firms are anything they use in the production process, e.g.

- Land
- Labour
- Capital

5.2 Output

Output is what a firm produces. It's useful to understand these terms:

Total output – this is the total quantity of the product produced by the firm. It's also known as total product.
Average output – this is total output divided by a total input, e.g. labour. It's also known as average product.
Marginal output – this is the addition to total output by using an extra unit of an input, e.g. labour.

5.3 Short-run and long run

Short-run (SR) – this means the time period when at least one factor input is fixed, e.g. in a factory more employees might be hired to increase output but they have to use the same stock of plant and machinery.
Long-run (LR) – this means the time period when all factors of production can vary, e.g. it's possible to go out and buy new machinery or set up new factories.

By their nature the SR and LR are not fixed time periods in economics. They vary from one firm to another, and one industry to another. As a rough guide you might say the SR is about 6-12 months and the LR anything above this.

5.4 Returns to scale

This is the change in percentage output as a result of a percentage change in all the factors of production. There are three possibilities:

Increasing returns to scale – the percentage change in output is larger than the percentage change in inputs
Constant returns to scale – the percentage change in output is the same as the percentage change in inputs.
Decreasing returns to scale – the percentage change in output is smaller than the percentage change in inputs.

5.5 The law of diminishing returns

Definition – the law of diminishing returns states that as you add a variable factor of production, e.g., labour, to fixed quantities of other factors, marginal output will at first rise but then fall.
Explanation - marginal output rises at first because each new worker can take advantage of specialisation and the division of labour. However, after a certain point diminishing returns set in and each new worker produces less than the previous one because communication, motivation and organisation suffer. Increased numbers of workers working on the same amount of fixed resources mean that the marginal output of each new worker goes into decline at some point, e.g.

- Agricultural workers in a field
- Barmen in a pub
- Workmen digging a ditch

5.6 Types of cost

Fixed costs (FC) - these are costs that do not vary with the level of output, e.g. rent, light and heat, insurance. If we draw them on a graph we get a straight line.

Theory of the firm

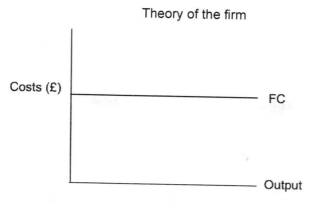

Average fixed costs (AFC) – this is fixed costs divided by total output. If we draw them on a graph we get a downward sloping curve as the fixed costs are being spread over a larger volume of output.

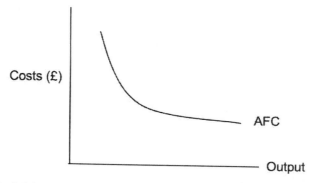

Variable costs (VC) - these are costs which vary with the level of output, e.g. wages, raw materials. The total variable costs (TVC) curve is s-shaped because of the law of diminishing returns. Sometimes you might see it drawn as a straight-line; this means VC per unit are assumed to be constant.

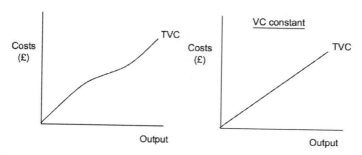

Theory of the firm

Average variable costs (AVC) – this is total variable cost divided by total output. If we draw them on the same graph as average total costs (ATC) they will be below them at every level of output. The vertical distance between the two curves represents the average fixed cost (AFC).

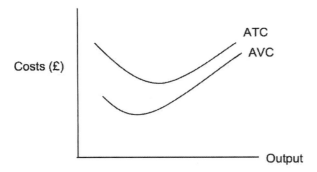

Total costs (TC) - this is the total cost of production and is equal to fixed costs plus variable costs (TC=FC + VC). It's s-shaped starting where the FC begin. If VC per unit are assumed to be constant it will be a straight line.

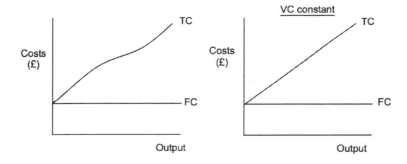

Average total costs (ATC) - this is total cost divided by total output. If we plot it on a graph we get a U-shaped curve showing that economies and then diseconomies of scale are taking place. We saw this in 2.3 above.

Marginal cost (MC) - marginal cost is the cost of producing an extra unit of output. Because we are looking at SR situations it's made up of the variable costs of production, i.e. materials and labour. If we draw it on a graph we get a J-shaped curve. Marginal costs fall then rise because of the law of diminishing returns.

Theory of the firm

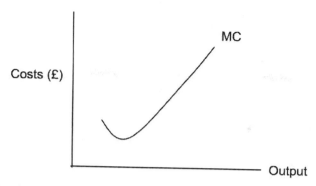

5.7 Calculation of marginal cost

Marginal cost is the cost of producing one more unit of output, e.g. in the table below the marginal cost of producing the second unit is 25-20 = 5. The FC=10. Another way of expressing it is to say that it's the difference in total cost at successive levels of output.

Output	TC	MC
0	10	-
1	20	10
2	25	5
3	27	2
4	28	1
5	34	6
6	41	7
7	51	10

5.8 The relationship between MC and AC

An important point to remember when drawing MC and AC curves is that MC will always pass through the minimum point of the AC curve. We can reason this as follows. If MC<AC then AC must still be falling, but if MC>AC then AC must be rising. From this it must be true that MC will pass through the minimum point of AC.

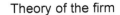

Theory of the firm

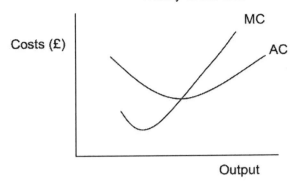

Costs (£)

MC

AC

Output

5.9 The relationship between MC and FC

Marginal costs are not affected by changes in fixed costs. This is worth remembering because it has been examined on a few of the recent multiple-choice questions. This is because we are only looking at the SR and in the SR only variable costs change not FC.

5.10 Relationship between SRAC and LRAC curves

In the LR a firm can vary all factors of production and so as it increases its scale it can reduce its AC. The SRAC curves are drawn inside the LRAC curve demonstrating as the firm expands it moves from one SR situation to another. Each situation, e.g. $SRAC_1$ represents an increase in scale.

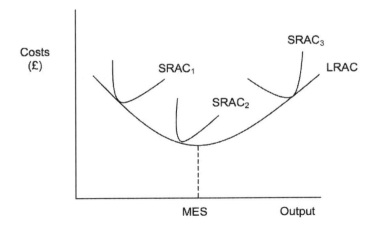

Costs (£)

$SRAC_3$

$SRAC_1$

LRAC

$SRAC_2$

MES

Output

The minimum efficient scale (MES) is the minimum output level required to reach the lowest LRAC. In the diagram above it would be the bottom of the LRAC curve. If the LRAC curve were basin shaped it would be where the flat section begins.

5.11 Revenue

Total revenue (TR) – this is the total sales revenue for the firm. It's equal to price times quantity (PxQ). If price is constant the graph will be a straight line through the origin. This is the case in what's known as perfect competition where the demand curve is perfectly elastic (see 8.1). If price is falling (as for a standard demand curve) it will be an inverted parabola with sales being maximised at its peak (MR=0). This is the case in imperfect competition, e.g. monopoly (see 9.2).

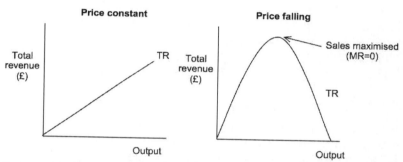

Average revenue (AR) – this is total revenue divided by total output. Because AR gives us the price at any level of output it's the same as the demand line. Therefore we can say AR=D.

Marginal revenue (MR) – this is the addition to total revenue of selling an extra unit of output. If we plot it on a graph we find that it is a straight line twice as steep as the average revenue (AR) line and goes through the x-axis. It can therefore be both positive and negative. See below.

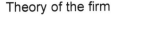

Theory of the firm

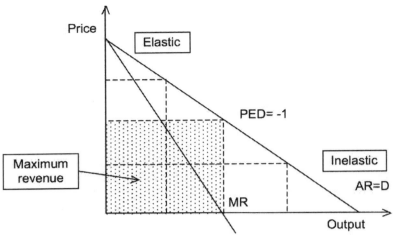

The reason why it can be both positive and negative is because TR increases and then decreases as you go down the demand curve. We can see this from the diagram above. TR increases up to the point where PED= -1 and then decreases after this point. Therefore it must be both positive and negative. This is also why we get the inverted parabola for TR shown previously.

From this diagram we can also conclude that TR will be maximised where MR=0. This is because if MR>0 then TR must still be increasing but when MR<0, TR must be decreasing. Another important point to remember is that when TR is maximised PED= -1

5.12 Calculation of marginal revenue

Marginal revenue is the increase or decrease in total revenue at successive levels of output e.g. in the table below the marginal revenue of the third unit would be, 45-35 = 10.

Theory of the firm

Output	TR	MR
1	20	20
2	35	15
3	45	10
4	50	5
5	50	0
6	45	-5
7	35	-10
8	20	-15

5.13 Profit, normal profit, supernormal profit and marginal profit

Profit – this is total revenue minus total costs. A firm will make a profit at any point where AR>AC.
Normal profit - this is the minimum amount of profit an entrepreneur would want to make in order to keep him in his present business. If he wasn't making this he would take his resources elsewhere and invest in another business.
Supernormal profit - this is any amount above and beyond normal profit. It's also known as abnormal profit.
Marginal profit - this is the addition to total profit of selling an extra unit of output. It's the vertical distance between MR and MC at a unit of output.

5.14 Economic cost and accounting cost

It's important to realise the following distinction:

Accounting cost - when accountants talk about the total costs of production they mean fixed costs plus variable costs.
Economic cost - when economists talk about the total costs of production they mean fixed costs plus variable costs plus normal profit, i.e. they include the opportunity cost of production. This is important because in the diagrams you see in the section on market structures you need to remember that average costs already includes an element of profit - normal profit.

Motives for firms and loss minimisation

6

6.1 Profit maximisation

This is the main motive for firms.

Formula

MC=MR

Explanation

If MR>MC then it means the firm can increase its profit by producing and selling an extra unit of output. However, if MR<MC then the firm will be losing profit it produces and sells an extra unit of output. Therefore, the profit maximisation point must be where MC=MR.

Graph

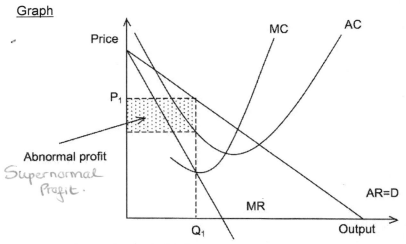

Abnormal profit
Supernormal Profit.

Reasons for profit maximisation

- Survival – without profits the firm cannot survive.
- To build more market share and/or gain market leadership – higher profits means a firm can put more into investment and marketing and it makes them stronger.

- To increase rewards to shareholders - higher profits means a firm can increase its dividend. It also increases the share price.

6.2 Sales revenue maximisation

Another possible motive for firms is to maximise their sales revenue. They might do this when there is a price war or they want to build market share at the launch of a new product.

Formula

$$MR=0$$

Explanation

If MR>0 then total revenue can still be increased if a firm produces and sells an extra unit of output. However, if MR<0 then total revenue will decrease if a firm produces and sells an extra unit of output. Therefore, total revenue must be maximised when MR=0.

Graph

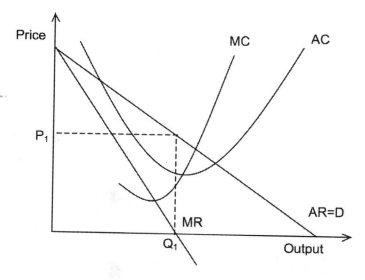

Reasons for sales revenue maximisation

- To increase market share
- To enhance the prestige and image of the company – bigger companies get more trust from customers and therefore more sales.
- Personal interest of the chairman and directors – their bonuses may depend on sales targets. Increasing market share may also enhance their personal prestige and career prospects.
- To deter new entrants by making the market seem less profitable than it really is.

6.3 Sales volume maximisation

This means maximising the number of units sold. The constraint is that the firm needs to be making at least normal profit. The motives will be similar to those for sales revenue maximisation.

Formula

AR=AC

Explanation

If AR>AC then the firm will be making supernormal profit; therefore it can still afford to expand its output if it wants to sell more units. However, if AR<AC then the firm will not be making normal profit, and will be making a loss. Therefore, the sales volume maximisation point must be where AR=AC.

Graph

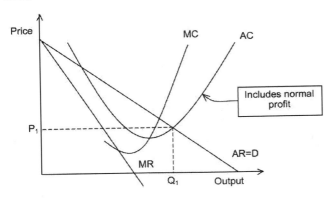

Reasons for sales volume maximisation

- To increase market share.
- To enhance the image and prestige of the company.
- Personal interest of the chairman and directors.
- To deter new entrants by making the market seem less profitable than it really is.

6.4 Profit satisficing

This means making just enough profits to keep the stakeholders in a firm happy, thereby allowing other motives to be pursued. There are three reasons why firms might do this:

Deter new entrants - if a firm is seen as highly profitable it might attract new entrants to the market and decrease profits in the long run.

Not to attract the attention of the CMA - a highly profitable firm might mean the market as a whole gets investigated. This could lead to fines and reduced profits in the future.

Directors' own interests - if the shareholders are happy they'll re-appoint the directors. This means the directors can pursue policies that maximise their own returns rather than those of the business, e.g. hitting sales targets to increase bonuses. Because the shareholders aren't involved in the day-to-day running of the business they won't necessarily see that the directors could make yet more profit.

6.5 Loss minimisation

Losses occur at any point where AR<AC. The loss minimisation point is where MC=MR.

Graph

Motives for firms

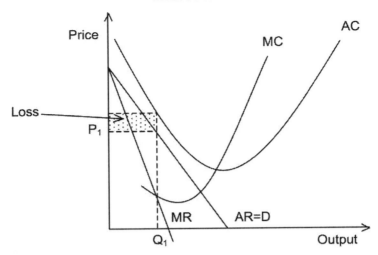

6.6 Break-even point, SR shut down point and LR shut down point

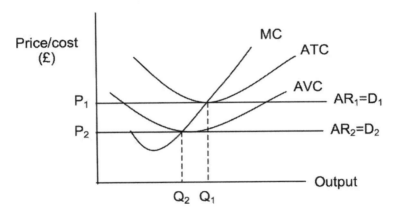

Break-even point (BEP) – this is the point where a firm is making neither a profit nor a loss. It's where total revenue is equal to total costs or AR=ATC ($P_1 Q_1$)

SR shut down point – this is the point where the firm can no longer cover its variable costs and make a contribution to covering its fixed costs. It's the point where AR is less than or equal to AVC (P_2, Q_2). Notice that in the short-run a firm would still keep producing between prices P_1 and P_2 because they can pay off part of their fixed costs and will be hoping that demand will pick up in the near future and make them profitable again.

Motives for firms

LR shut down point – this is the point where a firm will make a loss in the long-run. It's given by P<LRAC.

Types of efficiency

7

7.1 Allocative efficiency

Definition

This means scarce resources in the economy are allocated according to consumer preferences and maximises their economic welfare. In an individual market it occurs when price is equal to marginal cost (P=MC).

Formula

$P=MC$

Explanation

If P>MC then consumers are sending a signal to the market that they want more of that good to be produced (since price is a measure of how much they value the product). However, if P<MC then consumers are sending a signal to the market that they want less of that product produced. The point of allocative efficiency must therefore be P=MC.

Graph

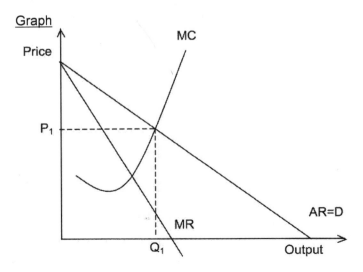

Types of efficiency

7.2 Productive efficiency

This occurs when a firm is producing at its lowest average cost. It's the point where economies of scale have been maximised. See point A on the diagram below:

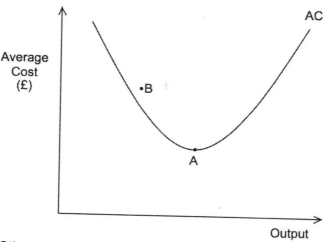

7.3 Other types of efficiency

Technical efficiency - this occurs when for any given level of output a firm is using the minimum number of inputs. Confusingly the term is sometimes used interchangeably with productive efficiency although strictly speaking it's not the same thing.

X-inefficiency - this occurs when a firm is not being technically efficient. It's any point above and inside the AC curve. It's also known as 'organisational slack'. See point B on the diagram above.

Dynamic efficiency - means resources in the economy are allocated efficiently over time. For an individual firm it means looking at how a firm could improve their productive efficiency over time, e.g. investment in new technology, introducing new management methods.

Pareto efficiency - this means a situation where it's impossible to make one person better off without making another person worse off. An example would be being on the edge of the production possibility frontier (PPF).

Technical and pareto efficiency are not on the syllabus, they are mentioned here only because they have occasionally come up on the multiple-choice answers in the past, although they've never been the correct answer.

7.4 Exam tips on efficiency questions

Efficiency questions on the data response section of the exam are fairly frequent, but often badly answered by students. The trick is to remember that these questions are basically about prices and costs. Allocative efficiency is the code word for 'prices' and productive efficiency is the code word for 'costs'. What you should be basically looking for is why prices may go up or down, or why average costs may go up or down. Usually it boils down to factors such as economies of scale or collusion. It's best to concentrate on allocative and productive efficiency, as there's usually enough to discuss just with these, but you can also bring in X-inefficiency or dynamic efficiency where appropriate.

Evaluation

For the evaluation think about these points:

- If you've been arguing that allocative or productive efficiency would improve think about factors from the passage as to why it may get worse.
- Cost cutting to achieve productive efficiency may mean a lower quality product or cuts to the service.
- Cost cutting may lead to an increase in AC in the SR, e.g. redundancy costs
- Cost cutting may have a social cost, e.g. higher unemployment
- Cost cutting to improve allocative efficiency may not mean lower prices - could just result in higher dividends for shareholders.

Market concentration ratio

8

<u>Definition</u>

This is the amount of market share held by the leading companies.

<u>Example</u>

UK tour operators	Market share (%)
Thomson	27.0
Airtours	16.5
First Choice	12.5
Cosmos	5.5
Thomas Cook	4.5
Others	34

In this example the 3-firm concentration ratio would be 56%; the 4-firm concentration ratio would be 61.5%.

Market structures

9

9.1 Perfect competition

(i) Market characteristics

- There are many buyers and many sellers none of whom have the power to influence the price of the product on their own.
- All firms and customers have perfect knowledge of the market – there is no information failure.
- All products are homogeneous, i.e. identical.
- There are no barriers to entry, i.e. there is complete freedom of entry and exit.
- There is perfect mobility of all factors of production – all factors of production can be switched easily between different lines of production.
- All firms are profit maximisers.

(ii) Examples

In the real world perfect markets don't exist because the conditions are so strict. However, good approximations are:

- Foreign exchange markets, e.g. dollar, pound, and yen.
- Agricultural markets, e.g. carrots, potatoes.
- Commodity markets, e.g. tin, copper, zinc, wheat.

In all these markets there are many buyers and many sellers, the products are nearly identical and entry costs are not high. Of them, the foreign exchange market is probably the best example as it's the only one where the products are truly homogeneous.

(iii) Purpose of the perfect competition model

Because perfect competition is strictly theoretical its real purpose is that it tells economists and policy makers what conditions you need to get the best resource allocation. All other types of market structure, e.g. monopoly, monopolistic competition, are referred to as imperfect competition because they are more or less deficient compared to it.

(iv) Demand curve

The demand curve for perfect competition is perfectly elastic. This is because all the firms only have a small amount of market share and all the products are identical. This means that each firm is a "price taker" and has to accept the price set by the market and can't determine it themselves. See below:

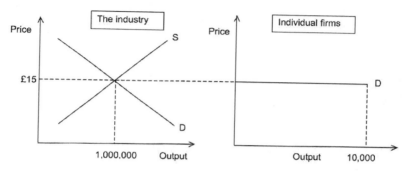

(v) Short-run equilibrium (SR)

The situation for firms in short-run equilibrium in perfect competition is shown below:

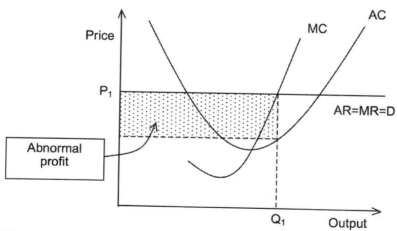

There are three characteristics to note:

- The firms can make abnormal profits
- The firms are allocatively efficient (P=MC)
- But the firms are not productively efficient

(vi) Long run equilibrium (LR)

In the LR in perfect competition supernormal profits get competed away. This is because there are no barriers to entry and all the products are the same. This means that new firms can easily enter the market and it shifts the supply curve for the industry to right and the demand curve for the individual firm downwards, thereby eliminating abnormal profit. See below:

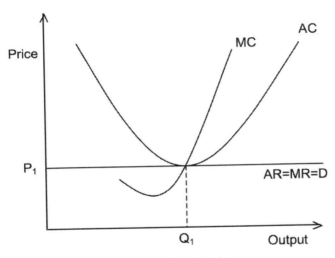

There are three characteristics to note:

- The firms can only make normal profit
- The firms are allocatively efficient
- The firms are technically and productively efficient

9.2 Monopoly

(i) Market characteristics

- There is only one firm in the market.

- Barriers to entry are high and prevent the entry of new entrants.

An important point to remember is that the legal definition of a monopoly is much less strict. It only requires market share of 25% or above.

(ii) Demand curve

Monopolies face a downward sloping demand curve. This is because they are the only firm in the market and their demand curve and the demand curve for the industry must be one and the same thing.

(iii) Constraints on the monopolist

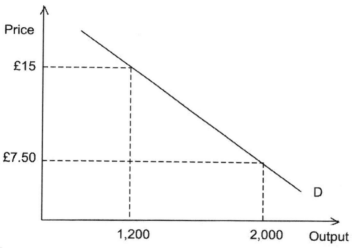

Contrary to common perceptions, monopolists *do* have constraints. They can set the price (they are "price makers") or the output level but they can't set both. In the diagram above we can see the monopolist can sell 2,000 units at £7.50 but they couldn't sell 2,000 units at £15. At that level only 1,200 people would buy them. Because of this the monopolist is said to be constrained by the demand curve.

(iv) Short-run and long-run equilibrium

Market structures

For a monopoly the SR and LR are the same thing because they are the only firm in the market. We can illustrate the situation on the diagram below:

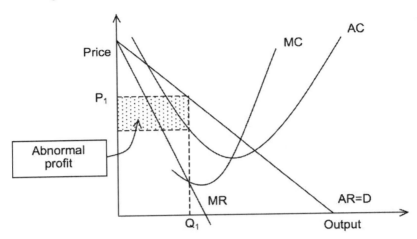

From this we can say three things about monopolies:

- The firms are not allocatively efficient (P≠MC).
- The firms are not productively efficient.
- The firms can make abnormal profits in both the short and long run.

As we would expect there is a misallocation of resources and market failure occurs.

(v) Natural monopolies

These are markets where there are very high fixed costs and where competition would be wasteful or inefficient. Examples are the railways, water, electricity and gas. In these situations it would be very inefficient to have two or more companies with different sets of infrastructure. See below:

Market structures

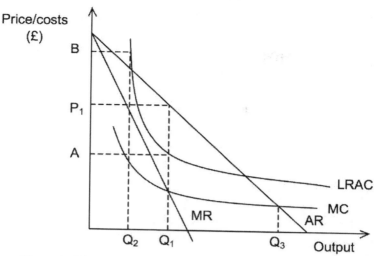

A profit maximising monopolist would produce at point Q_1 but splitting the output between two companies (Q_2) would not help because this would raise the average cost from A to B. Therefore consumers would suffer higher prices. The allocatively efficient point is Q_3, where the firm is making a loss (AR<LRAC), and this is why these types of firms are often state owned or at least state regulated.

(vi) Problems of monopolies to firms, consumers, employees and suppliers

Firms

- Firms become complacent and inefficient. Eventually it could lead to their demise as they get over-taken by market changes and new competitors.

Consumers

- Higher prices, less choice, lower quality – because there is a lack of competition monopolists will profit maximise (MC=MR) and therefore set prices well above the allocatively efficient point (P=MC). It also means there is reduced choice for consumers and there is no incentive for the monopolist to improve the quality of service/goods they provide.

- Price discrimination – monopolies may use price discrimination to increase profits. This will reduce consumer surplus for some customers.

Employees

- Less jobs - a profit maximising monopolist will produce at an output level below the allocatively efficient point. This means less workers will be needed than the ideal situation.

Suppliers

- Monopolists may use their market power to push down prices for suppliers.

Economy

- State monopolies may waste resources by undertaking cross-subsidisation to keep otherwise unprofitable services afloat, e.g. rural railways. They also require subsidies which pushes up taxes.

(vii) Benefits of monopolies to firms, consumers, employees and suppliers

Firms

- Higher profits and bigger dividends for shareholders
- Higher profitability means the firm can maintain its international competitiveness assuming those profits are put to good use.

Consumers

- Lower prices - big firms can get full economies of scale and reduce the price.
- More investment – abnormal profits means the monopolist can invest more and therefore improve the quality of the service and products, e.g. pharmaceuticals, banking, telecommunications, television, computing.
- Cross-subsidisation – in natural monopolies (state monopolies) it means profitable parts of the service can subsidise unprofitable parts of the service, thereby

ensuring access for all, e.g. rural railway service, universal letter delivery.
- Price discrimination - means lower income consumers can access the good or service, e.g. railways.

Employees

- Higher profitability might mean higher wages
- Job security - a more profitable firm might mean more expansion and job security.

Suppliers

- Maintenance of contracts - a monopoly might have little interest in shopping around for the best deal and so keep on using inefficient suppliers who might otherwise have gone out of business.

9.3 Monopolistic competition

This occurs when there is many firms in an industry each selling a slightly differentiated product.

(i) Market characteristics

- There are many firms in the market.
- Products are differentiated – either by product features or branding and advertising.
- Each firm has a small degree of monopoly power and makes decisions independently of other firms in the market.
- Barriers to entry are low.

(ii) Examples

The best examples are shops on your local high street, e.g. local restaurants, hairdressers, bakeries, newsagents, take-aways.

(iii) Demand curve

The demand curve for monopolistic competition is downward sloping but more elastic than it is for monopoly because there is more competition.

(iv) Short run equilibrium

This is similar to monopoly, the only difference is that as noted the demand curve is more elastic. See below:

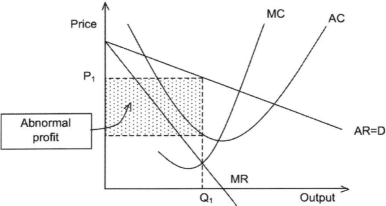

The three key characteristics to note are:

- The firms can make abnormal profits.
- The firms are not allocatively efficient (P≠MC).
- The firms are not productively efficient.

(v) Long run equilibrium

In the LR a lack of barriers to entry means that the supernormal profit gets competed away. The demand curve shifts to the left and becomes tangential to the AC curve. See below:

Market structures

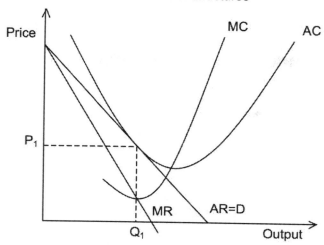

From this we can see three things:

- The firms are not allocatively efficient (P≠MC).
- The firms are not productively efficient.
- The firms can only make normal profit (AR=AC).

9.4 Oligopoly

This is a market that is dominated by a small number of large firms.

(i) Market characteristics

- Market concentration ratio is high - supply is concentrated in the hands of a few firms.
- Decision-making is interdependent – this means firms take into account the possible reaction of competitors before making pricing and output decisions.
- Barriers to entry are high, e.g. initial costs, branding and advertising costs.
- Firms prefer non-price competition, e.g. advertising and branding, design and packaging. Price competition, and price wars, are seen as likely to reduce revenue, and so should be avoided. In any instance non-price competition can also be used to build barriers to entry, and so preserve the firm's position within the oligopoly.

- Price rigidity and periodic price wars – prices are usually rigid but then price wars break out to test where the price level is.
- Price leadership – there is often price leadership, one firm initiates a price change and others follow it.
- Collusion and anti-competitive practices are relatively common, e.g. predatory pricing, price fixing and market sharing agreements.

<u>(ii) Examples</u>

Just think about your main shopping high street and the big providers of manufactured goods and services, e.g. supermarkets, banks, cars, pharmaceuticals.

<u>(iii) Demand curve</u>

The demand curve for oligopolies is kinked. See below:

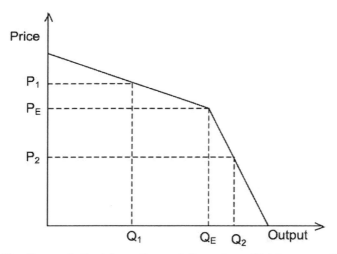

The theory is that firms fear raising prices (P_1) because they think no one will follow suit, and consumers will switch to cheaper rivals. If that happens, the belief is that it would lead to a fall in market share, and a decrease in total revenue. At the same time they fear lowering prices (P_2), because they think other firms will follow suit, creating a price war, in which market share does not increase significantly. If that happens, again, the belief is that it will lead to a fall in total revenue. This implies the demand curve is elastic above the current price level, and inelastic below it, therefore it must be kinked. This is why prices are said to be "sticky" or rigid.

(iv) Oligopoly and collusion

Collusion means firms acting in such a way as to avoid strong competition. There are two types, open collusion and tacit collusion. Open collusion means firms openly fixing prices, output or having market-sharing agreements. Tacit collusion means this is all done in an unspoken way. Collusion as we've already seen is illegal.

Collusion is relatively common in oligopoly for three reasons:

- **High market concentration ratio** – this means it's relatively easy to manage the secrecy, as there are only a few firms involved. It also increases the inter-dependence of decision-making so the firms see the benefit of acting together like a monopoly to maximise their profits.
- **High barriers to entry** – this means that a few large firms continue to dominate the market and keeps the situation stable.
- **Collusion is often difficult to prove** – unless the collusion is open there's usually a lack of evidence it's actually happening. Furthermore, firms can often offer plausible excuses when challenged, e.g. similar cost structures might explain similar prices.

For a more detailed examination of collusion see section 10.0

(v) Collusion and game theory

When we talk about collusion what we usually mean is price fixing. Game theory can be used to explain why firms in oligopoly do this. The syllabus says you can explain it using the prisoners' dilemma or a normal pay-off matrix. Both are explained below.

Prisoners' dilemma

Market structures

Prisoner X

		Deny	Confess
Prisoner Y	Deny	1 Each gets 6 months	2 X goes free Y gets 5 years
	Confess	4 X gets 5 years Y goes free	3 Each gets 2 years

If we imagine two prisoners locked up in cells, unable to communicate with each other then the optimum solution for them is obviously option 1 - each gets 6 months. The problem is they can't collude and so both will probably confess and get 2 years each - option 3. This is called the Nash Equilibrium. The relevance this has for oligopoly, is that in the real world collaboration between firms is usually possible so they can see there's an incentive to collude.

Pay-off matrix

Below is a pay-off matrix for two firms in oligopoly.

Firm A

		High price	Low price
Firm B	High price	1 Each gets £50m	2 Firm A gets £60m Firm B gets £25m
	Low price	4 Firm A gets £25m Firm B gets £60m	3 Each gets £40m

The independent decisions are options 2, 3 and 4. The firms are likely to choose option 3, because each is afraid their rival will undercut them and try to make the maximum amount of money possible, £60m. Because this results in each only getting £40m, there is therefore an incentive to collude, and price fix with a high price, because that way each gets £50m. This is known as a maximin strategy because each firm maximises their minimum payoff.

Having said this the situation is always unstable, because each firm still knows they can get even more money, £60m, if they *do* undercut their rival. This explains why price fixing often ends in price wars in the long run. The stability of the collusion depends on such factors as PED, barriers to entry and whether there's a recession.

(vi) Useful terms to remember in game theory

- Dominant strategy – the best strategy for a firm irrespective of what other firms do.
- Maximin – a strategy by which a firm seeks to maximise its minimum gains.
- Maximax – a strategy by which a firm seeks to maximise its maximum gains.

(vii) Oligopoly and efficiency

Firms in oligopoly are likely to be allocatively and productively inefficient because they are profit maximisers. This means they will set the price above the allocatively efficient point (P=MC), and their costs will be above the minimum AC (MC=AC). Having said this, there are some evaluation points we can raise:

Evaluation

- Having a few big firms could still be more efficient than having lots of small firms - lots of small firms could mean no firms can get full economies of scale. That would lead to higher AC and higher prices, i.e. productive and allocative efficiency would be worse.
- Having a few very profitable firms could mean more investment takes place - this is better for innovation and therefore consumers. This is particularly important in technological and scientific industries, e.g. pharmaceuticals, TV, banking.

- It's difficult to tell how inefficient oligopolies are - because knowing where the allocative and productively efficient points are in a market is not that easy to determine.
- How inefficient an oligopoly is depends a lot on the competition authorities - if they are vigilant then the inefficiencies can be minimised.

9.5 Contestable markets

(i) Definitions

Contestable market - this is a market where there are low barriers to entry and exit. This creates a constant threat of new entry and only normal profits can be made in the long run.
Exit costs – these are the unrecoverable costs of entering a new market, e.g. advertising and some of the initial costs. They are also known as sunk costs.

Contestable market theory is based on the idea that when firms are deciding to enter a market they are not just concerned about how much it costs to enter, they are also concerned about the minimum they will lose if they have to leave the market early. This is represented by the exit costs.

(ii) Market characteristics

- There may be one or many firms.
- Barriers to exit and entry are low – this creates a constant threat of new entry.
- Firms genuinely compete against each other and there is an absence of anti-competitive practices.
- Only normal profits can be made in the long run.
- "Hit and run" tactics – low entry and exit costs may mean it's profitable for firms to enter the market for a short time and then leave quickly once competition increases.

(iii) Assessing market contestability

This has become a favourite exam question. The things you should look for are:

- **Likely size of entry and exit costs** – if these are high it would tend to indicate the market is an oligopoly not a contestable one.
- **New entrants** – if there have been new entrants recently this suggests entry and exit costs are not that high and the market is contestable.
- **Low profitability** – this implies strong competition and therefore market contestability.
- **An absence of anti-competitive practices** – this implies genuine competition and therefore market contestability.
- **Impact of new technology and the Internet** – this lowers the entry and exit costs and increases the likelihood of contestability.
- **Short-run vs. long-run** - market may be contestable now, but in the LR could become oligopoly as more firms join the market and firms see an incentive to collude.
- **Low concentration ratio** - this implies competition is strong and reduces opportunities for collusion.
- **Strength of new entrants** - potential new entrants may already have strong brand names and economies of scale so can break into the market relatively easily, e.g. foreign car makers in US car market.

<u>(iv) Examples</u>

A good example of a contestable market is the airline industry. There have been large numbers of new entrants recently suggesting the entry and exit costs can't be that high, e.g. Ryan Air, EasyJet, BMI. Other markets that have become much more contestable are:

- Banking
- Music and other media retailing
- Publishing
- Travel agents

All of these industries have been much more affected than most by the impact of new technology and the Internet. These have greatly reduced location, distribution and production costs and therefore entry and exit costs. The so-called "weightless products", e.g. music, film and newsprint, have been particularly susceptible to new entrants.

9.6 Monopsony

(i) Definition

Strictly speaking monopsony exists when there is only one buyer in the market. On a practical level we speak of monopsony power when a firm or group of firms has a dominant buying position in the market.

(ii) Examples

A good example at the moment is the monopsony power that supermarkets, such as Tesco and Sainsbury, have over farmers and food suppliers.

(iii) Effects on monopsonists, suppliers, consumers and employees

(a) Monopsonists

Increased profits – monopsonists can use their market power to force the suppliers to reduce their prices. This reduces their costs and increases their profits.
Increased rewards for shareholders – higher profits means an increase in dividends for shareholders.
Increased investment - higher profits means the firm has more money left over for investment. They can use this to build further barriers to entry and reinforce their market dominance.

(b) Suppliers

Lower profits – because of weak bargaining power suppliers may have to reduce their prices and therefore profits will fall.
Exit from the industry – some firms will have to leave the industry because they are no longer profitable. Others may switch to other products or concentrate on a narrower range of products in the hope they can get economies of scale and stay in business, e.g. farmers faced with the monopsony power of the supermarket giants like Tesco, Sainsbury's and ASDA.
Unemployment – if firms leave the industry or have to cut costs this will lead to unemployment.

(c) Consumers

Lower prices – if the monopsonist can negotiate lower prices from suppliers they may pass this on to consumers.
Reduced choice – monopsony power often results in suppliers concentrating on fewer products. This is because by doing so they can get economies of scale, reduce their average costs and maintain their profitability.

(d) Employees

Job losses – if suppliers leave the industry or have to cut costs this will lead to job cuts.

Collusion and cartels

10

Collusion means firms acting together in such a way as to avoid strong competition. There are two types of collusion:

Open (overt) collusion – this is where firms openly fix prices, output or have market-sharing agreements, e.g. by exchange of e-mails. Also known as forming a cartel these are illegal in the UK, EU and many other countries.

Tacit collusion – this means having an unspoken agreement to fix prices, output or divide up a market, e.g. price leadership. Much more difficult to prove this is also illegal in the UK.

10.1 Conditions that make collusion and price fixing more likely

High market concentration ratio - this makes collusion and price fixing more likely because of two reasons:

- First, the firms will see if they join forces they can act like a monopoly and maximise their profits. It increases the inter-dependence of decision-making, and firms will therefore see the benefits of acting together. We saw this in game theory.
- Second, it makes communication easier – with fewer firms it makes it easier to manage the secrecy.

Barriers to entry are high - this helps to keep the market concentration ratio high.

Firms can trust each other not to cheat – this keeps the agreement stable.

Substitutes unlikely to be developed in the short-run - this reduces competition and keeps the situation stable.

Demand for the product is increasing or stable – again this helps keep the market stable.

It's difficult for the authorities to discover if there is a cartel – if it's easy to keep it a secret this will encourage collusion.

10.2 Difficulties encountered by cartels

Cheating - because the business environment is constantly changing, firms in the collusion may be tempted to cheat to gain extra revenue and profits.

Legislation - in most countries price fixing and collusion are illegal, e.g. in the UK and the EU firms can be fined up to 10% of their turnover.

New entrants - the existence of abnormal profits means the market will attract new entrants who may not be willing to go along with the agreement.

Development of substitutes – new competitor products are a constant threat to collusive behaviour, e.g. biofuel is becoming an effective substitute for oil.

Changing market conditions - e.g. recession. Sudden changes in demand can destabilise agreements.

10.3 Effects of collusion and price fixing on firms

Positive

- Firms can gain abnormal profits in both the SR and LR.
- These profits can be used to build up further barriers to entry through investment, innovation (R&D) and marketing.
- The abnormal profits can be used to increase rewards to shareholders, i.e. dividends.
- Higher profits mean a higher share price – this should make it easier to attract further investment.

Negative

- Firms who collude and price fix may get less competitive in the LR if they get complacent and don't use the abnormal profits wisely, e.g. investment, training and R&D.
- Collusion and price fixing may encourage competitors to innovate and improve and therefore lead to the LR decline of the firm.
- Collusion and price fixing may lead consumers to look for substitutes – therefore profits fall in the LR.

10.4 Effects of collusion and price fixing on manufacturers

- Higher costs, e.g. oil – OPEC
- Search for cheaper substitutes – to avoid high prices.

Collusion and cartels

- Look at ways of reducing costs if input costs rise substantially, e.g. relocation of factories overseas, redundancies, investment, and training

10.5 Effects of collusion and price fixing on consumers

- Higher prices for consumers – reduction in consumer surplus.
- Search for cheaper substitutes in the LR.

Price discrimination

11

Price discrimination means charging different prices to different market segments for the same good or service, e.g. rail travel, underground, air travel.

This is also known as third-degree price discrimination. You do not need to know first-degree or second-degree price discrimination for the syllabus.

11.1 Conditions necessary for successful price discrimination

- Barriers to entry are high and the firm has a degree of monopoly power
- There are identifiable market segments each with a different PED, e.g. children, adults, pensioners
- The firm must be able to keep the market segments separate at relatively low cost and to prevent resale of the product from one market segment to another. This is called market seepage.

11.2 Techniques used to keep market segments separate

- Time of day – rail, underground, cinema, airlines
- Geography – cars
- Age – underground, buses, rail

11.3 Theory

The theory behind price discrimination can be explained in two ways:

(i) Consumer surplus

Price discrimination

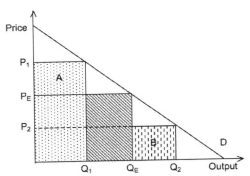

In the diagram above if the firm had only charged P_E then they would have only gained P_E x Q_E as their revenue. However, if they charge P_1 to the wealthy customers and P_2 to poorer customers they can increase their revenue by area A and area B. As long as the costs of policing the price discrimination (e.g. photocards) are below the extra revenue gained, profits will increase.

(ii) Three sector diagram

This shows that a firm can increase their abnormal profit if they segment the market rather than charge everyone the same price. See below. In sub-market A demand is elastic, in sub-market B demand is inelastic if we add together the abnormal profits from both markets it's clearly greater than just from the total market alone:

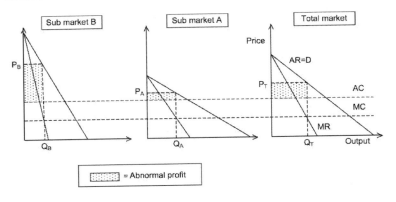

11.4 Evaluation

- Cost of keeping market segments separate need to be lower than extra revenue gained for price discrimination to increase profits.
- Competition can undermine the effectiveness of price discrimination.
- Not always easy to set prices for each market segment - situation is dynamic and it's not an exact science.

11.5 Advantages and disadvantages of price discrimination to consumers

Advantages

- Higher profitability of firms means more money available for investment - firms can improve quality of good or service.
- Lower income consumers can now access the product, e.g. students, pensioners - air travel, rail travel.
- Profits can be used to cross-subsidise other activities, e.g. profits from business mail helps Royal Mail maintain the universal postal service.

Disadvantages

- Higher profits may just mean higher dividends for shareholders.
- Some consumers now have to pay higher prices and others may find the service more inconvenient, e.g. early morning/late evening travel times.

Pricing and non-pricing strategies

12

12.1 Pricing strategies

(i) Cost-plus pricing

Definition

This means adding a set profit margin to the total costs per unit.

Example

If a company manufactures a product for £1.40 and adds a cost-plus percentage of 25% to arrive at the final selling price, the final selling price would be:

$$(£1.40/100) \times 125 = £1.75$$

Advantages

- It means that the firm will always be able to cover its costs and make a profit.
- For some businesses it may be the only way of pricing a job because the costs are uncertain, e.g. construction, aircraft manufacture.

Disadvantages

- It's inflexible – if there is a lot of competition the firm may lose sales because they aren't prepared to lower their prices.
- If the firm miscalculates its costs the price may be uncompetitive.

(ii) Predatory pricing

Definition

This means a firm setting their prices below the AC of weaker competitors in order to force them out of the market.

Pricing and non-pricing strategies

Advantages

- The firm can capture market share and expand.
- In the LR the firm can increase their revenues and profits by putting the price back up once weaker competitors have left the market.
- Enhances the firm's image and reputation by having a bigger market share.

Disadvantages

- Problem of brand loyalty - even with cheaper prices consumers may still not be willing to switch.
- It's illegal and the firm could get a hefty fine if the competition authorities discover it.
- The firm could make substantial losses in the SR.
- May damage the image of the product – it may make it look cheap.
- May condition customers to expect cheap prices in the future.
- Only works if PED is elastic – the market needs to be price sensitive.

(iii) Limit pricing

Definition

This means setting prices below the predicted AC of new entrants in order to deter them from coming into the market. The idea is to sacrifice some profit in the SR to be able to make higher profits in the LR.

Advantages

- Increase revenues and profits in the LR – the firm can put prices back up once the threat of new entry is over.
- Maintain the image and reputation of the firm as the market leader.

Disadvantages

- The firm loses profits and revenues in the SR.

- May condition customers to expect lower prices in the future.
- It's illegal – the firm could get fined if the competition authorities find out about it.

(iv) Price fixing agreements

Definition

This means colluding with other firms to fix prices. It's also known as forming a cartel.

Advantages

- Firms in the cartel can enjoy abnormal profits – therefore they have more money to invest and build up further barriers to entry, e.g. advertising and branding, patents.
- Higher abnormal profits mean bigger rewards for shareholders and directors, i.e. dividends and bonuses.
- Higher abnormal profits mean a higher share price – this makes it easier to attract investment.

Disadvantages

- It's illegal – the firm could face a substantial fine.
- It may be difficult to maintain in the LR – situations change and cartel members might start breaking the agreement.
- It may encourage a complacent attitude – in the LR smaller more innovative competitors may break into the industry and break the domination of the large firms.

(v) Others

- Discount pricing, e.g. 'buy-one-get-one-free' (BOGOF), discounts for limited periods.
- Under-cutting rivals
- Sales maximisation
- Revenue maximisation
- Price discrimination
- Premium pricing, e.g. Stella Artois, 'reassuringly expensive'

12.2 Non-pricing strategies

Pricing and non-pricing strategies

(i) Advertising and branding

Advantages

- Increases demand – therefore increases revenues and profits.
- Strengthens brand loyalty
- Can be used to develop unique selling points (USP's) and product differentiation.
- Makes demand more inelastic – therefore it's easier for the firm to control prices and profit margins.

Disadvantages

- Costs – advertising campaigns are not cheap. Can the firm afford it?
- Brand loyalty - difficult to get consumers to switch.
- Effectiveness – it may be difficult to target the market precisely. It's best used for mass-market products.
- Opportunity cost – it maybe better to spend the money elsewhere, e.g. investment, training.

(ii) Improving quality and service

For example in the airline industry this would be providing:

- Bigger seats
- Better food
- In-flight entertainment

Advantages

- Relatively cheap way of "adding value".
- Can be used to develop product differentiation and USP's.

Disadvantages

- May not be that cheap – particularly for businesses with low profit margins.
- May not be that effective – the competition can quickly copy you.

(iii) Takeovers & mergers

Advantages

- Eliminates competition and increases market share
- Increased market power – easier to control prices
- Increased economies of scale – therefore falling AC and increased profitability
- Increased profitability means more money left over for investment – therefore can improve product quality and spend more on branding/advertising

Disadvantages

- Cost of merger/takeover
- Diseconomies of scale – may mean rising costs. Only about 50% of mergers/takeovers succeed.
- May not be allowed by CMA – substantial lessening of competition

(iv) Others

- Merchandising and display, e.g. locate confectionery near check-out for impulse buying, attractive in-store display
- Market sharing agreements
- Loyalty cards, e.g. nectar cards
- Packaging
- 'Buy-one-get-one-free' – increases consumer loyalty
- After sales service, e.g. important in car industry – breakdown, maintenance.
- Online ordering
- Trade exhibitions
- Product redesign
- Investment in new technology to increase productivity and reduce costs

Privatisation

13

13.1 Definitions

Privatisation – this means returning the nationalised industries to the private sector, e.g. water, gas, electricity and the railways.
Deregulation – in general terms this means reducing legal restrictions on businesses. In the context of privatisation it means opening up markets that were once state or local authority monopolies to competition, e.g. buses, post office.
Nationalisation - this means taking a private sector business into government ownership, e.g. railways.

13.2 Structure and organisation of the privatised industries

The general principle adopted by the government has been to separate the infrastructure from supply. This is because the running and maintenance of the infrastructure is a natural monopoly, while the supply of the good or service is not. Therefore the government has let one company (or companies) run the infrastructure and let other companies compete for the supply. We can see this in the examples below:

Railways – Network Rail (formerly Railtack) runs and maintains the infrastructure and Train Operating Companies (TOC's) run the rail services. There are about 25 of these including well known names like Virgin Rail, Heathrow Connect and First Great Western.
Gas – the infrastructure is maintained by the National Grid (formerly Transco) and gas suppliers supply gas to households. These include companies like E.ON, British Gas and EDF energy.
Electricity – the companies are split into three groups – generators, distributors and suppliers. Generating companies create the electricity, distributors maintain the infrastructure and get the electricity to households and suppliers supply the electricity to customers. The suppliers may be the same as gas suppliers (duel-fuel suppliers) or different. Examples include Southern Electric and NPower.
Water – there are about 15 water companies that both maintain the infrastructure and supply customers. These are organised on a regional basis and include companies like Thames Water and Severn Trent.

Telecommunications – BT maintain the telephone network and telephone suppliers supply the calls, e.g. Talk Talk, Virgin.
Post Office – business delivery has been completely opened to competition and there are now some 60 licensed operators, e.g. TNT, UK Mail, DHL. Private door-to-door delivery is still a Royal Mail monopoly.

13.3 Regulation

Because the privatised industries would be prone to collusion and market abuse the government has appointed a regulator for each industry, e.g.

- Gas and electricity – OFGEM
- Water – OFWAT
- Telephones – OFTEL

The regulator acts like a pseudo-competition to make sure the market works efficiently. It does this by using price capping and performance targets.

(i) Functions of the regulator

The regulator has four functions:

- To encourage firms to be more efficient - allocatively and productively
- To maintain and improve the quality of the service
- To control prices and prevent consumer exploitation
- To ensure firms carry out sufficient investment

(ii) Price capping

The regulator controls prices using a price cap. The price cap limits the price increases the firms in an industry can make each year. The regulator works this out by using the formula RPI-X where RPI stands for inflation and X stands for the efficiency gains the regulator thinks the firms can make, e.g. if the RPI was 5% and X was 2% then the firms would only be allowed to increase prices by 3% the following year. What it means is that prices fall in real terms each year.

Benefits

- It creates an incentive for firms to increase both their allocative and productive efficiency - real price cuts force the firms to move closer to the allocatively efficient point (P=MC) and also incentivise them to reduce AC by more than X.
- Prevents consumers being exploited with high price increases
- Price cap is usually in place for 5 years - so allows firms to plan ahead.

Drawbacks

- It may create a barrier to entry – if the price cap is too tough profits will be low and this could mean no new firms want to enter the market decreasing competition.
- If the price cap is generous it allows firms to make abnormal profits, and it could be in place for up to 5 years.
- Regulatory capture – this means firms persuading the regulator to 'go soft' on their industry and set a favourable price cap and/or easy performance targets. This would disadvantage consumers.
- Cost cutting may effect quality of the service - the drive to cut AC may mean a cut in services, e.g. Royal Mail has now stopped second deliveries.

(iii) RPI+K

Rather than price capping the regulator may also allow price increases above inflation if he thinks this is justified. In this case he will use the formula RPI+K, where K stands for the permissible price increase above inflation. Examples of situations why this might happen are:

- Regulator may think the industry requires new investment to maintain the service, e.g. water industry
- Change in legislation that means increased costs

(iv) Performance targets

These are usually to do with improving the quality of the service, e.g. punctuality of trains, reducing customer complaints, water leakage. These may or may not be linked to a system of fines to create a financial incentive.

(v) Quality standards

These are similar to performance standards but focus on a general level of service rather than giving a specific target that can be measured, e.g. Royal Mail has a legal obligation to maintain the universal postal service.

(vi) Profit regulation

This is stated on the syllabus but is only a proposal at the moment. It has been used in the USA, but it has several flaws. The way it works is that firms are only allowed to make a certain rate of return (profit) based on their capital stock. Whilst this could be used to keep prices down, it encourages firms to overstate their capital stock and make wasteful investment. Regulatory capture is also a problem.

13.4 Contracting out and competitive tendering

Contracting out – this means the government or local government getting private sector firms to produce goods and services for people rather than organising and providing it themselves, e.g. refuse collection, street cleaning
Competitive tendering – this means the government or local government getting private sector firms to bid for contracted out public sector work.

(i) Advantages

- Lower costs for taxpayers – because the private sector will do the work more efficiently than the public sector.
- Higher quality product/service – because the private sector has the expertise to do the job better.
- More efficient use of resources – because private sector has to compete for the work and therefore won't waste resources.

(ii) Disadvantages

- Safety issues – in order to maximise profits private sector firms may do a low quality job. This may cause injuries and accidents, e.g. railways.
- 'Bid rigging' - firms can collude to share contracts among themselves while putting on the appearance of competing with each other.

13.5 Public private partnerships and the private finance initiative

Public private partnerships (PPPs) – these are projects that use a mixture of public and private finance to provide a public sector good or service. The most common form of PPPs is the Private Finance Initiative (PFI) another is partial privatisation.

Private finance initiative (PFI) – this means the government getting a private sector company to build and maintain a piece of public infrastructure and then leasing it back from the same company on a long lease. Examples include building schools, hospitals and roads, and London Underground maintenance.

13.6 Advantages and disadvantages of PFI

(i) Advantages

- Lower costs for taxpayers
- Higher quality product/service
- Reduced government borrowing – because the government is leasing the asset and paying off the debt over a number of years.
- More efficient use of resources

(ii) Disadvantages

- May be expensive – private sector firms have often negotiated very favourable terms with the government/local government. 'Bid rigging' has also been a problem.
- Cost of borrowing - because the firms doing the work are in the private sector they have to pay higher rates of interest than if the government borrowed the money themselves. This pushes up costs.
- Widens income inequalities - trade unions criticise PFI because it gives an incentive to firms to cut wages to increase profits and/or win contracts.

- Hides true extent of government borrowing – PFI repackages what is government debt as private sector debt. This distorts the government's borrowing figures.

13.7 Government intervention and economic efficiency

There are various ways in which government intervention can promote economic efficiency. The most obvious ones are:

- Price capping, e.g. RPI-X
- Privatisation, e.g. business postal delivery
- Competition policy, e.g. fines, investigating anti-competitive behaviour
- Contracting out
- PFI

If you go back and look through the relevant sections you'll see how these tie in with promoting allocative and productive efficiency bearing in mind what was said in section 6.4.

The labour market

14

14.1 Factors affecting demand for labour

Demand for the product - labour is a derived demand. If demand for the product increases then the demand for the labour that makes the product will increase as well. Similarly any changes in the conditions of demand will also affect the demand for labour, e.g. changes in prices of complementary and substitute goods; changes in taste and fashion; changes in income.

Changes in technology - the substitute for labour is capital, therefore if new technology becomes available this can make jobs redundant and reduce demand.

Prices of other inputs - if there are increases in the price of raw materials, or overheads, this will increase costs and may reduce demand for labour.

Productivity – if productivity increases this will make the firm more profitable. Hence demand for labour will rise.

Legislation and employment regulation - e.g. increase in NMW, employment legislation making it easier to hire and fire workers.

Wage rate – fall in wage rates reduces costs so firms are more likely to hire workers.

14.2 Factors affecting the elasticity of demand for labour

Ease of substitution of capital for labour - the easier it is for firms to substitute capital for labour the more elastic the demand curve for labour will be. This is because it gives firms more of a choice. The increased competition makes the demand curve more elastic.

The time period under consideration - the more time you have available to find and train workers the more elastic demand will be.

Elasticity of demand for the product - labour is a derived demand. If demand for the product is elastic, then the demand for the labour that makes that product will also be elastic.

14.3 Factors affecting supply of labour

Birth rates and death rates - this determines future labour supply.

Migration - immigration and emigration determines how many people are coming into and leaving the country, e.g. in 2015 total immigration was 630,000 and total emigration 297,000. Therefore net migration was 333,000

Training - determines how many people are employable.

Income tax - determines how attractive it is to work.

State benefits - determines the incentive to work, e.g. JSA, housing benefit.

The National Minimum Wage (NMW) – determines the incentive to find a job and join the labour market.

Trade union power – can determine wage rates and therefore the incentive to work. It can also affect demand and create unemployment – see 14.5 below.

Social trends – in the post-war period it has become socially acceptable for women to work. This has dramatically increased their participation rate and increased the labour supply.

Legislation - can determine how attractive it is to work and also labour costs,

e.g. Equal Pay Act, Health and Safety at Work Act.

14.4 Factors affecting the elasticity of supply of labour

Skill level - where the skill level is low supply will be elastic because it's easy to train workers and it doesn't take very long, e.g. cleaners. However, if the skill level is high then supply will be inelastic because it's hard to train workers and it takes a much longer time, e.g. doctors.

Labour mobility – this applies to both geographical and occupational mobility. If it's easy to move around the country and find work, or it's easy to switch from one job to another because of transferable skills or good training programmes, it will make supply of labour more elastic. A more detailed examination is in section 14.7 below.

Time span under consideration - supply is always linked to time. In the short run it tends to be inelastic because it takes time to train people. In the long run it becomes more elastic because you have more time to train people.

Availability of migrant labour - this will make the supply curve more elastic because the workers have already been trained. There is therefore no waiting period before they join the workforce, e.g. labour from the new EU accession countries like Poland, Lithuania, and Estonia.

14.5 Wage determination and labour market equilibrium

Labour market

As with any other market, wages are determined by the interaction of supply and demand to produce an equilibrium wage rate. See below:

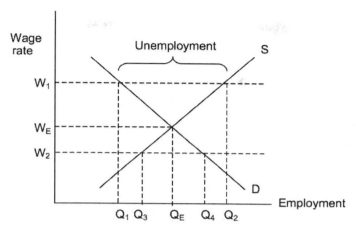

The equilibrium wage, above, is W_E. If wages are too high, e.g. W_1, it will increase the supply of labour relative to demand and create unemployment of Q_1 to Q_2. If wages are too low, e.g. W_2, then demand for labour will be higher than the supply of labour, creating a shortage of workers of Q_3 to Q_4. The market won't clear until wages are at the wage rate equilibrium.

14.6 The National Minimum Wage (NMW)

The NMW is the legal minimum wage employers have to pay. It came into force in 1999 and depends on age. There's one for the over 21's, another for those 18-20, and a further one for the under 18's.

Advantages

- **Provides an incentive to work** - it reduces unemployment and helps to keep people off benefits. It makes the opportunity cost of staying on benefits less attractive.
- **Increased productivity** - an NMW provides extra motivation for workers and raises productivity levels.
- **Reduces poverty** - an NMW raises the income of the poor and reduces income differentials.

Labour market

- **Increases spending** - an NMW means people have more money to spend. This creates a multiplier effects across the economy.
- **Encourages firms to invest more** - the increase in labour costs means firms may invest more to raise productivity and reduce their labour costs.

Disadvantages

- **Could increase unemployment** - if the NMW is set above the equilibrium wage (W_E), see below:

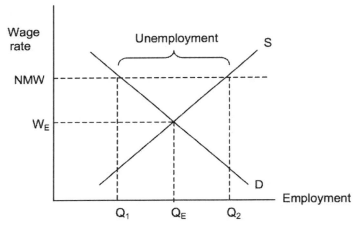

- **Could make firms less competitive** - an NMW raises firm's production costs. This could affect the UK's international competitiveness.
- **Could cause inflation** - if firms try to maintain profit margins by raising prices because of rising wage costs.
- **Knock-on effect to other workers** - higher paid workers may demand pay increases to maintain pay differentials. This could cause wage inflation.
- **May not tackle poverty** - beneficiaries of the NMW are not just the poor, they include working mothers as well as students and young people still living at home. These people are not poor but they still benefit. Another problem is that you can't benefit from the NMW unless you have a job in the first place.

14.6.1 Factors affecting what effects the NMW has on firms

- **Proportion of total cost taken up by those being paid below the NMW** - if this is low, then firms might hardly notice anything at all, e.g. supermarkets vs. solicitors.
- **Proportion of total cost taken up by labour costs** - some firms are capital intensive. The labour intensive firms will suffer more than the capital intensive firms, e.g. cleaners vs. software consultants.
- **Ability to pass on extra costs** - if demand for the product is inelastic then the firm might be able to pass on the extra costs to consumers without making redundancies.
- **How higher paid workers react** - if higher paid workers react by demanding pay increases then the firms will be more affected than if they don't.
- **Ability to exploit the workforce** - people on low pay may not be aware that the NMW exists or be in a position to argue with their employers because they fear they will lose their job. Therefore employers can exploit them and keep wages low, e.g. illegal workers.

14.6.2 Factors affecting the amount of unemployment the NMW could create

(i) How much the NMW is above the equilibrium wage

The further the NMW is above the equilibrium wage (W_E), the greater the amount of unemployment created. See below:

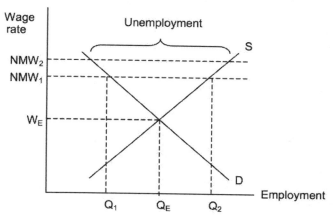

Compare NMW_1 with NMW_2.

(ii) The inelasticity of demand and supply of labour

The more elastic demand and supply of labour are, the greater will be the unemployment created if the NMW is set above the equilibrium wage. See below:

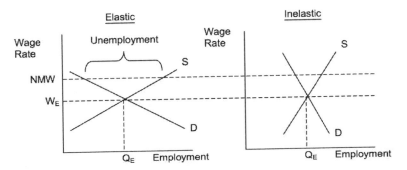

14.6.3 Maximum wages

The syllabus makes reference to maximum wages: this means a wage ceiling on what people could earn. This has been proposed to limit Chief Executives pay and also bonuses of bankers working in the city. The feeling is that they have been exploiting their positions to maximise returns to themselves. The arguments against it would be that it's difficult to implement and those key workers would just go to other countries creating a 'brain drain'. It could also reduce economic growth because the UK could lose its most productive workers.

It would be more possible for the government to set maximum pay limits in the public sector, because it has monopsony power there, e.g. doctors, nurses. This could keep public spending down, but the problems are the reaction of unions and strikes, and the effect on public services as result. It could also create a brain drain as in the private sector, or workers would just simply transfer their skills to the private sector.

14.7 Labour immobility

Labour immobility creates market failure because it means workers find it difficult to move from one job to another. There are two types of labour immobility – geographical immobility and occupational immobility.

14.7.1 Geographical immobility

This means the ease with which workers can move around the country to find work.

(i) Reasons for geographical immobility

House prices – the gap in house prices between north and south is now so large people can't move south even if they wanted to.
Family and social ties – people are reluctant to move because of family and social ties. They might also not want to move because they don't want to uproot their children from good schools.
High percentage of home ownership in the UK – this acts as a disincentive to move, as it's easier to move if you rent. It contrasts with the much higher proportion of rented accommodation we find in other EU countries.

(ii) Policies to overcome geographical immobility

Improving transport links – i.e. road and rail links. This would cut journey times for workers and make it easier for them to take jobs further away from home.
Relaxation of planning laws – which enable construction firms to build housing, especially on green belt areas and the southeast of England.
Increasing the construction of social housing – such as council properties and housing associations. Low rents are more affordable than mortgages.
Housing subsidies for key workers where prices are high – e.g. nurses and teachers. Subsidies may include mortgage relief, shared ownership and relocation grants. The problems here have been long waiting lists, and many of the available homes have been in undesirable areas.
Improving the operation of job centres - so that more information is available on jobs available in an area

14.7.2 Occupational immobility

This means the ease with which workers are able to change jobs.

Labour market

(i) Reasons for occupational immobility

De-industrialisation – the continuing switch from a primary and secondary industry based economy to one based on the service sector has meant that many low skilled manual workers have found themselves without jobs.
Insufficient education, training, skills and work experience – due to failures in the education system and lack of vocational courses

(ii) Policies to overcome occupational immobility

Training schemes – especially for the unemployed, e.g. New Deal. This might include subsidies to private sector companies to offer trainee placements. The problems have been the quality of the training schemes, and also that many people can't afford to spend their time in training rather than at work.
Increasing provision of further education – especially vocational courses post-16, so that school leavers are more employable and flexible.
Increasing provision of higher education – there has been a dramatic increase in higher education, but criticism from employers as there has been a lack of vocational courses, e.g. too many people doing Madonna Studies. There have also been problems over access caused by student loans and tuition fees.

14.8 Public sector wage setting

Wages in the public sector are set by the government, and they have monopsony power. Effectively, workers have to accept what the government offers unless they have strong union representation or are prepared to transfer their skills to the private sector.

You should also be aware of the interaction between the public sector and private sector in terms of the labour market. There are three things you should note:

- If wages are higher in one than the other, then it will encourage workers to transfer between the two.
- The public sector can influence how productive the private sector is, e.g. if wages are higher in the public sector, the

best people will transfer there, weakening the private sector.
- The government plays an important role in managing expectations of what pay increases should be, and therefore the effect on inflation, e.g. if public sector pay only rises by 2%, private sector employers often use this as a benchmark to limit their own pay increases.

14.9 Current labour market issues

Things that you should be aware of are this:

- The total amount of workers in the public sector is about 5.3 million (ONS 2015). This is about 17% of all people in work.
- Public sector job cuts have been estimated at about 1 million between 2010-15 (ONS 2015). This was part of the government's austerity strategy to bring the budget deficit down. In terms of the labour market, it's increased supply in the private sector, and contributed to keeping wages down generally.
- The government introduced the National Living Wage (NLW) in 2016. It applies to those 25 and over, and currently stands at £7.20.
- The Living Wage Foundation campaign group sets the UK Living Wage at £8.25, and the London Living Wage at £8.40. It's voluntary and about 2,000 businesses have signed up for it including HSBC and GSK.
- Public sector employment is uneven around the regions. It's lowest in London at 15%, but highest in the Northern Ireland at 26% (ONS 2015). A useful evaluation point to remember is that the effect of public sector employment, and public sector job cuts, varies regionally.

Index

Price Capping

Firms which have monopoly
power can be regulated
e.g. OFCOM, OFWAT

RPI − x

RPI = 5% (inflation)

x = level of efficiency
savings deemed to be
possible by regulator

x = 2%

RPI − x = 3%

Real terms = −2% (prices lowered)

RPI + Y

RPI = 5%

Y = level of price
increase sanctioned by
the regulator

why?

① Investment → ↑ Quality

② To cope with
new legislation

RPI + Y = 6.2%

↑

Consumers benefitting
↳ Worse quality?

consumers not benefitting but
better quality?